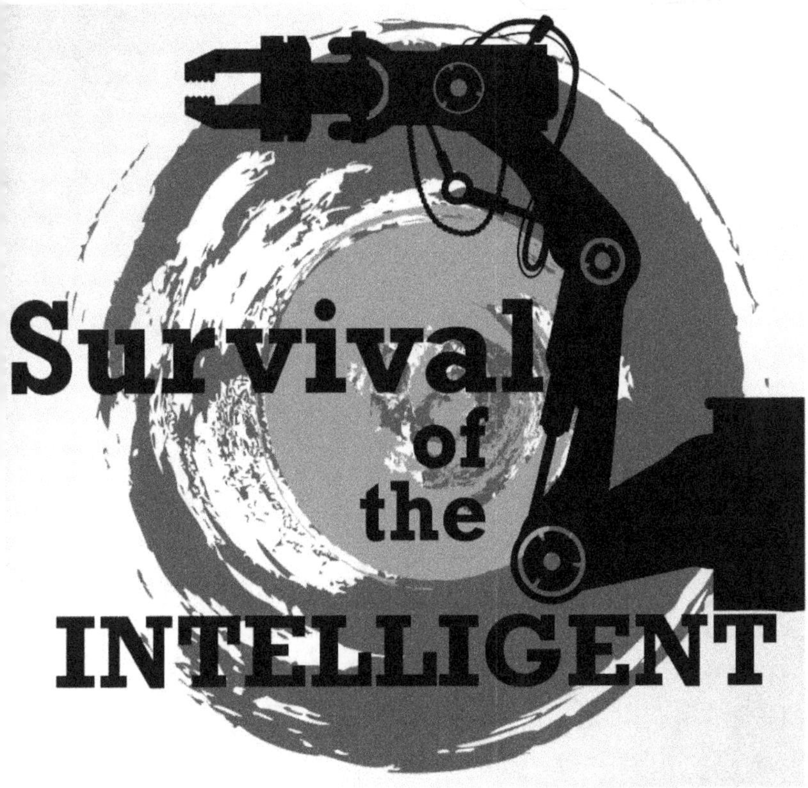

Survival of the INTELLIGENT

A Guide to Surviving the Future and following your passion post-2015

Table of Contents

Wake up, World! The Future is Now!

We are on the brink of a huge social change, years in the making. This change is inevitable, and no one knows what the final outcome is going to be. --As a whole human race, we aren't quite ready for this, in fact, most of us don't even see that it is happening right in front of our eyes.

Let me illuminate the reasons *why change is happening*, and then we can talk about *what is happening*.

Why change is happening:

1. **Globalization**

    In the next 5 minutes, you can own a product that took someone, halfway around the globe, **hours** to create. Not only that, but it cost them next to nothing to produce that product and you sustain their lifestyle for one more day by your paltry purchase. --hop on itunes, google play, amazon music, or some other music distribution platform and purchase an indie song or movie and you'll know what I mean.
    Digital products are available to us instantly the moment we purchase them--they don't have to be reproduced every time you buy them. Other

products can be reasonably available and in our possession in less than a week; and many of these products are produced in other countries where the cost of living is lower and resources are more readily available and cheaper. In the past, buying something from across the world required a fortune to ship it overseas, but these days globalization means a cheaper product, and available in less time.

The ramification of globalization on your life is not only that products are suddenly available to you that previously were difficult to get ahold of or took a long time to do so, but it is also that jobs are being outsourced to the cheapest bidder anywhere in the world. Whether you support purchasing only from locally owned and run businesses, you are forced to consume products that were made on a global market.
Take for instance the concrete on your street, the rubber on your tires, the steel, copper, and plastic in whatever electronic device you are using to read this, or the paper on which you are reading this book--it wasn't all made in one spot. It wasn't all mined in one country, and furthermore, the people involved in creating it didn't live down the street from you and may even be from another country.

From a social evolutionary perspective, the people who are willing to do the task for the cheapest price, but perform up to the expected level of quality are always going get the work, be able to pay their bills, and survive. Those who can't perform at the expected level of quality or who can't do it at the cheapest price will remain jobless, and eventually go extinct.

2. **Automation and Robotics**

People have feared robots since the dawn of their creation. Robots have taken many jobs that humans could not do up to the expected level of quality or for the cheapest price. No, not sentient robots (yet), but automated machines. In the US, for example, car companies have cut jobs and installed assembly bots to attach screws, rivets and to assemble cars.--Humans lost jobs to those robots.

Furthermore, the field of robotics has advanced substantially. Robots are able to haul gear for soldiers across extreme terrain as well as enter buildings where there is the fear of explosion.-- Robots are taking risky jobs that humans don't want to do as well as manual labor jobs that people don't want to do at the price that robots are paid: virtually nothing.

And I'm not just talking about mechanical robots. Software is slowly eliminating the need to use paper for business records. That's one less paper plant and all the jobs that it provided. It's also one less intern to sort the records.

In sum, robots are taking a large share of jobs that humans could be doing. What that means for you, or perhaps for your children (if you're already retired) is that the number of jobs available is becoming less and less. What's left of the job market are menial jobs that businesses don't see the point of creating a robot to do, such as fast food cashiers and cooks.--Sure, robots could do it right now, robot vending machines could be made that deliver food to the customer's car, and machines already exist to brew your latte, steam your rice, and fry your hamburger, etc.; but what's the point if they can pay you less than it costs to build the robot to do the job in the present market?--All that will change however, as the price of robots drop! Just wait!

Do you understand where I'm going with this? Okay, one more...

3. **Availability of Tools**

Tools are a big part of what separates us from animals. Tools make an impact on the world and allow humans to do things that no other living creatures can do.

Because of robots and because of globalization, you have the benefit of greater access to tools. The computer, tablet, or cellphone that you might be reading this on is a tool. Without robots to build it for you, or people who will build it cheaply, you wouldn't have this tool. Even if somehow it was available to you, it would cost a fortune without cheap labor and/or robots.

The internet is a tool. You can use that tool to gain access to useful information. Furthermore, the internet can be used by businesses to gain information about you, such as your browsing habits, shopping habits, and creepily, your gps location. Yes, privacy has gone out the window! Tools that were previously unknown 10 years ago are suddenly available to everyone who knows how to utilize them.

As far as the future is concerned, tools work for you and against you. The people who have the right tools, know how to use them, and are at the right place and time, are the ones who get the job, make money and get ahead. Since everyone can get those tools, you have to be ahead of the game and plan in order to be at the right place and at the right time with your tools, otherwise someone else who is more prudent will do just that and you'll miss out on the opportunity. In short, you will not survive.

Now do you understand **what is happening**? Piece those 3 reasons together: Globalization, Automation (Yes, Robots), and Open Access to Tools.

What is happening:

Adding these three together you get our present economy; one full of angry people who are intelligent, are capable, and are willing to work, but still aren't getting good jobs because they still need to earn enough money to live on or pay for the things they desire most. Without a good enough job, they struggle to survive and they are angry. They're angry because when they were born, people could make a career out of starting at the bottom and moving up the ladder and they could invest in a low-cost education and accelerate to the top;--but once those people were old enough to enter the workforce, things were different. Now, education is no longer enough, and people who start at the bottom usually stay at the bottom and watch as the bosses' friends and family--people who don't deserve the promotion--surpass them for every career advancement.

Maybe you're one of these people, sitting there at the bottom? Or maybe you walk past neighborhoods where people live who apparently have money-- they have the good life, or at least a better life than yours, and you wonder why and how are they able to do it?

A good friend of mine once quoted to me, "It's not that there aren't jobs, it's that there aren't good jobs."--Yes, that's the issue isn't it! Anyone can wash windows and most people can do that job well or learn it quickly, but not everyone can live off of the salary of a window washer; furthermore, a lot of us would feel debased for having to do such a simplistic task and be paid next to nothing to do it our whole lives--especially after we worked so hard to develop our skills and personality and see it wasted in that way.

There is a major problem with where our human race is headed, and perhaps you are intelligent enough to see it: Those who have access to robots, or have access to factories throughout the world, or even have access to all the tools are the ones who are surviving. Those people appear to be free. They can do whatever they want, whenever they want. They can choose to pay you low wages if they want to because if you don't take their wages or play by their rules, they'll pay someone else, halfway across the world, to do it for less. Eventually, they won't even need humans because they can build machines to do practically everything for them.

This is the future--this is the present! If robots continue to be made--which they will--every human being will be out of a job except for the managers of those robots. Those people will be free and you will be stuck forever doing the dirty work in a job you hate, for a boss you dislike, for wages less than you are worth, and probably they will live halfway across the globe and not care much about what happens in your little town or your life in general.

It seems to me that our problem lies not in how the world works--because trust me, if you were benefiting from this future world then I'm sure things would be spectacular!--The problem is how we have been trained to think about life as a continual progression from start to finish, when we should really be thinking about life is as a giant leap forward, over a vast chasm that separates those who are successful from those who never take the leap and keep thinking they can put one foot in front of the other and eventually they'll find a path to the other side. --It does not work that way. So, with the rest of this book, I'm going to present to you the correct way that you should be thinking about life--living--in our post-whatever world, and this mindset will help you take that leap to not only success but also stability, safety, and a whole lot more freedom.

Your Future Job Prospects

In the very near future--actually, right now--this very moment, there are only about 7 jobs that humans can fill. Plato, back in 400 BC (more than 2000 years ago), argued that there are only really 3 jobs, but I'm going to stretch that out a little bit to help you understand. Those jobs are:

1. Inventor-Engineer
2. Artist-Designer
3. Manager-Decision Maker
4. Accountant-Asset Quantifyer
5. Lawyer
6. Politician
7. Salesperson

Yes, yes, a couple of these are redundant and if you want to know what Plato said, read the book The Republic. Also, you could add "Police or Soldier" to our list but I'm avoiding that prospect because I'm sure you've considered that career already and decided that it's too dangerous or risky and you want to live a more peaceful life. Besides, robot drones and high tech profiling surveillance cameras are slowly taking away some of those jobs anyway...

Back on subject, I want you to picture a world where everything is run by robots. What will humans do with all that spare time? They won't have to work because a robot will do all work for them. Robots can't do everything though--they can't create, they can only recreate; so if you want to listen to music it'll have to be composed by a human. They can't make original decisions, so the best they could do is read back to you a list of suggestions that you yourself wrote for yourself. They can't differentiate between things that are available and things that shouldn't be available, -- those are called "bugs" in computing terms, so as far as the robot is concerned if something is there, it's there, even if it should not be, and if it's not there, it's not there, even if it should be. Again, they can't make original decisions, so they can't write laws or present arguments for why a law that isn't presently regarded as "there" should be interpreted as being "there." And last of all, robots can't convincingly lie. Ever. They can only tell the truth about what they have been told; which, in simple words, means they can be programmed to lie, but anyone who knows how the program works will be able to differentiate between a lie and a truth--even if that means they have to make a seperate tool to do it. In this future, what will you do with your spare time other than sitting in a lawn chair eating food and gaining weight while robots do everything you could ever imagine?

The answer seems pretty simple, practical, and intelligent: Invent, engineer, create, make decisions, take inventory of everything, interpret hard questions, govern, and sell. The beauty is that these are the things that humans tend to inherently love and excel at anyway!

Engineer Some people love to invent, build and engineer. The job of an inventor-engineer is to *solve problems by creating solutions* in the form of products or services.--Well, sorta. I mean, you could even be an inventor-engineer even if what you created wasn't a product or a service, it was a "deliverable," (this is the technical term for a creation that someone asks for, including the creative work of dreaming up a process, or a name, or generating ideas, etc.). Inventor-engineers tend to specialize in a specific field, such as the field of robotics, or medicine, or architecture, or thingamajigs. Inventors have to be really knowledgeable about how things work, and in today's world (not necessarily the future), some of the most brilliant inventors had to spend 20+ years in schooling to get enough knowledge base in order to do their job...I'd say that's about to change however, because people like you are going to engineer a better education plan; especially now that you know that there are really only 7 jobs out there and can specialize education into producing humans capable of excelling at one of those 7 categories.

Artist Another thing that humans tend to love doing is to create stimulators--I'm referring to Art in its broadest form. Some people love to paint, others love to play music, others love to film videos, create video games, act, dance, tell jokes, and all around entertain others. I would even include athletes in this category because their work exists simply to stimulate other human beings either by motivating them or by triggering emotions insides of them such as awe, inspiration, or excitement.

At the root of all art is *stimulating others,* and we humans love to stimulate each other and be stimulated by each other. Humanity needs these people and they will need them even more once robots take all of our jobs and we have nothing to do or think about. Artists help us pass our time in enjoyable, meaningful ways, and I think that's a very noble calling in life.

Managers Unfortunately, managers will always exist. Unless of course you are presently a manager, then it's less unfortunate that your job will always exist. Actually, what we think of as the function of a manager will probably change the most out of any job with the more robots that we hire and the more humans we fire. What this job will really be doing is *making decisions.* I think that it is very likely that at some point we will all be managers to an extent in the sense that we'll all have at least a couple robots that we have to manage in order to do our main job.

The real function of the future decision maker will be to make decisions regarding where to invest present resources in order to preserve those resources and gather new resources if we choose to expand our operations. Managers also have to be a little prophetic in that they need to prepare and devise plans for how to deal with future complications that will arise or may arise.

It doesn't sound like much, but it's an exhausting job! Robots will constantly annoy them with emails and alerts and probably alarms will be going off left and right just to say things like "Water levels low! Water levels low!" "Power outage! Warning!" "Robot on fire! Calling Robot Fire Brigade!" Then, the good manager has to decide whether to repair the robot or scrap it and get a new one, and if so, where to get the new robot from: RoboRob or Robots-R-Us. And yes, some people LIVE for these kinds of jobs because they love making decisions and being held responsible for those decisions. They love making decisions even while others may feel anxious and panic at the thought of having to make a choice.

Accountants Still other people like to keep track of things. If a lowly robot errors out and somehow wanders out into the big city and gets lost, how will you know that you had that robot in the first place? If that robot's sole function is to water a bed of flowers in your garden and you have been so busy arting and managing and inventing that you haven't been to your garden in weeks, you probably wouldn't notice that it was gone. Even when you did notice it was gone, where will you get the parts to make a new one if you didn't already have the plastic and metal on hand to rebuild it? Accountants of the future are going to do much of the same things that accountants of the past have always done: *valueate the worth of assets, inventory them, and project guesses for how many or how much will be necessary in the future and when.* Yes, robots can do much of these functions, but robots have a hard time determining the worth of one lowly waterer robot in the grand scheme of operations without someone telling them specifically what that value is. To the unprogrammed robot, the worth of a gardener is as important as an assembly bot, but to you the gardener isn't your main priority.

Lawyers In the future, laws will still exist, and these days they definitely still exist. Laws are always flexible because language is flexible and subject to interpretation. In situations where the interpretation of laws can be confusing and create conflicts and disputes, sometimes it's better to step back and let someone else trained in interpretation and presentation gather the pertinent information and present it in a useful way to decision maker. This is the job of a lawyer--*to interpret the situation and argue for that interpretation over any other interpretation.*

Politicians Along with Lawyers, there will be politicians, though likely their role will be that of decision maker/manager. Politicians of the future will probably devote their time to deciding how to best use the present resources at hand as well as asking the question of, "what precedents can we set now to resolve future conflicts?" Again, those are questions that decision makers should be asking as well, so the two jobs go hand in hand. If you develop strong decision making/manager skills, you'll potentially do well in a political position.

Salespeople Lastly, there are salespeople. Salespeople use a mixture of skills to stimulate people--similar to what artists do--but with the sole purpose of getting others to buy into their product, idea, or service. Salespeople have to quickly *gauge the needs and wants of their customer, present how their product can fulfill that need, and guide them along to finishing up the paperwork and collecting the payment that initiates the exchange.* --This, of course, is oversimplified of the whole process, but it is something that robots can't fully do. Yes, robots can be programed to do these functions, but they would have to be programmed by a salesperson for each and every product, service, or deliverable. At some point, this becomes tedious and it's easier to have a salesperson sell rather than inventing robots that can sell for you, not to mention that many people love the thrill of selling and would fight very hard to make sure their job wasn't outsourced to robots.

In the real future--the one that is happening right now--you will probably have to be a little bit of everything, from inventor, artist, manager, accountant, salesperson, even politician and lawyer. Keep reading; I'll explain how that works in a moment...

Adapting to the Future

I get it, you're probably a little bit overwhelmed right now, and maybe you don't fully believe me that the future is now. Maybe you're sitting there thinking you have time--that you have 10 maybe 20 years before all of this will happen and that you'll be an old man or woman by that point and your bank will be full of money for you to live on for the rest of your life. Perhaps 10 years is all that you think it will take to get you to progress from flipping burgers to calling all the shots as a manager over other burger flippers. Or maybe you think someone will intervene in your case--some hero politician who swoops in to grant you free education, free healthcare, and free housing. Or maybe you expect a windfall--the death of a wealthy relative who is awarding you lots of money and then you'll be set for life?

To that, I say, "Good luck!"

The odds are stacked against you, and they were stacked against you from birth. If you're from any of the generations following the baby boomers, you missed your shot at progressively getting ahead. The way the world works now, in light of those three big important changes, is that if you don't take a leap to do something today, each day, you will get further behind.
You will fall behind either because you are

spending more money than you are taking in, or you aren't learning skills fast enough to catch up with your competition, or you don't have the physiological capability that others have and are able to do two or three times as much in a day as you are.

10 years from now, you don't want to be the last one to embrace this new life because you'll be too far behind to catch up. I feel for you--life's a struggle, and change is difficult, which is why I wrote this book. --Don't think that I'm doing this for purely selfless reasons--no, I expect you and I to mutually benefit one another. For starters, since you paid for this book, you helped me keep moving forward, but I expect more from you. I expect you to be a force for change in this world. We need to get everyone on the same page with where humanity's future is headed, and after you read this book it will be up to you to get your friends and family members on board with helping complete the evolutionary process.

What will I have to do to Evolve?

If you want to not only survive and be free, but also *thrive* in the next 10 to 20 years, you will need to do 3 things:

1. **Gain Experience**

   I'm sure you've heard this thrown around casually by countless people who pretend to know what it means. --Let me correct the years of lies they have told you by saying first, it does not mean get more schooling; second, it does not mean getting a job and working for someone else. What it means is get practice.
   Under the old rules of how life worked, you were expected to bounce from one job, or position, to the next until you had enough "experience" (i.e. time) under your belt to be promoted to manager or whatever your dream job was. --That didn't work then and it doesn't work now. For a decade or more, a huge push was made to increase schooling among young fools who companies and organizations said, "just lacked the experience for the jobs they needed to hire." --This prompted officials and universities across the globe to increase class sizes and accept more students into their programs.--But this also did not work.
   What was needed then, and what is needed now, is for people to gain real experience. Let me

explain this a different way: The difference between two musicians playing the same song comes down to which has more experience. You gain experience through practice, study and devotion. Some people learn things quicker than others and they can achieve the same level of experience in a lesser amount of time, but they still have to practice to get there. The world needs more people who practice and are intelligently learning, not people who stop practicing the moment they master the basics.

You might counter what I'm saying with, "Yes, but how do we get 'practice' if we don't have the job?" But working is different from practicing. Working is the application of experience you have already gained, practicing is experimenting through trial and error until you have trained your body or mind how to perform the correct way. Even still, your question is irrelevant: you're still thinking about how the world used to work rather than how it works now--and will work in the future. --As I stated earlier, you can't take step after step until you've arrived at the other side because there is no bridge--no one has the time to both build a bridge for you to follow AND make it across themselves.

Let me repeat myself: there are only 7 jobs out there. Pick one that you think you would be happiest with and study up on how to gain an abundance of the crucial skills related to it. Buy your own tools and make an attempt at it. Take a leap and hope that you can survive, because if you don't do anything and you let the next 10 or 20 years roll by hoping that things will work in your favor, you'll be disappointed when only a select few around you wisen up, gain those experiences, and get ahead of you.

The two easiest ways to gain experience are to study--which is mostly free thanks to the internet--and to practice, which can be done easily if you just purchase the tools you need to do it and start using them.

2. **Be Creative**

Your creativity is the only thing that others cannot take away from you or claim ownership of. Yes, they can lay claim on the products of your creativity, they can take your ideas, they can take your work, and they can pretend that they did it and not you, but they can't be the original creator once you already created it. The moment that you create something, that thing is yours forever. Creativity, then is one of the most valuable things in the universe. People who can consistently create things of worth for themselves and for other people are indispensable.

Creativity isn't hard. Every time that you speak, you are creating meaning out of a string of words--You essentially create things every day and you probably didn't realize that. Granted, some things are harder to create than others, but the way that we create things follows a very distinct pattern that I'm going to share with you. If you follow this pattern you will never be without ideas. Think of ideas as the blueprint or instruction manual. If you have the blueprint, you can create that blueprint into a tangible object, a digital object, or even create a copy of the blueprint and share it with others. Any time that you have to share an idea with someone you are creating a copy of that blueprint--the copy is written on the words that you speak about it. This book--a written out copy of my creative idea--is a tangible version of the blueprint I created, but before it reached you it had to be converted from the blueprint that I created and turned into whatever form you are viewing right now. Again, it went from creative idea, to blueprint, to its present state whether digital or print that you are looking at right now.--This will come into play later on in the book.

So what's the 'secret' pattern of creativity?

A. Have a Need
B. Be in an Urgent Situation
C. Flesh it out
D. Eureka!

You have to have a need to create something, otherwise there will be no reason for your mind to exercise its creative muscles. It's just like lifting weights, if your body hasn't ever been required to lift a certain amount of weights it will never develop the muscle needed to lift them. If you don't need to say something or you don't need to think something then you won't create any words regarding it and it will not exist until that need arises.

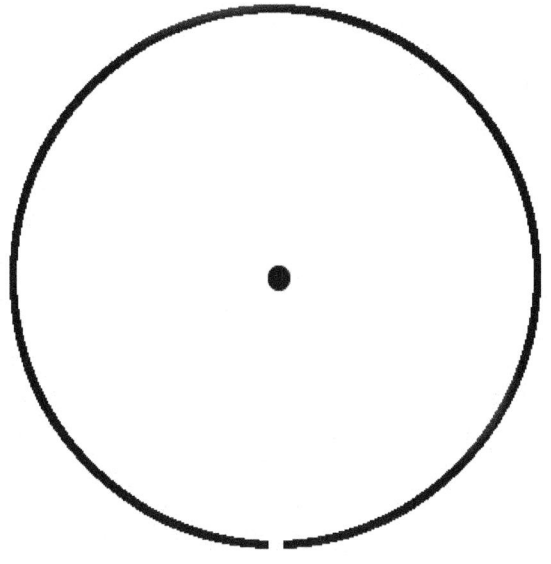

If you want to force creativity, start by setting up the need to create. Some people do this by looking for problems and creating solutions to those problems--the solution wasn't needed until there was a problem. Other people take this further and look for patterns and they see a problem with viewing the pattern as incomplete; that's what prompts them to create. Sometimes this is called, "closing the circle". If the outline of a circle stops just before it touches itself, you might be bothered by this, and think it's a problem, and therefore create a solution that closes that circle, either by creating something over top of it or drawing the circle the rest of the way, or turning it into something other than a circle. Even if you don't consciously complete the circle, your subconscious might complete it for you and upon first glance you will assume it is complete.

Having the need isn't enough though for more complex creative tasks. High school students understand this very well: when homework needs to be done but there isn't a deadline on it or the deadline is so far out that it seems irrelevant, the homework doesn't get done. It isn't until the night before the test or the day before it's due that we humans feel the urgency behind the task and so we come up with a solution for the problem and we cram to get the homework done on time.

If you want to force creativity, raise the stakes. The higher the stakes the more effort that your mind will put into being creative.

When I was about 12 years old I went on a fishing trip with my dad and a couple of his friends. The trip involved hiking 2 miles through steep, high altitude terrain through the forest between three small fishing lakes. It was very far from civilization in the High Uintas. At some point during the trip I separated from the group to go on ahead to the third lake but I wandered off the trail and got lost. It was a very scary situation and after realizing that I was lost, backtracking to see if I could find the trail again, and wasting my energy calling out in hopes that someone would hear me, I sat down briefly in the shade. My mind was frantic and started the creative process: I remembered the old saying, "every river leads to a lake or an ocean," and there aren't any oceans in Utah, so when I came across the next dry river bed I followed it downhill until it came to one of the lakes we were fishing at. Because the situation was critical, I found my mind creating all sorts of other possible solutions from climbing trees, building a shelter and waiting until search and rescue came, making my own trail makers and walking in a single direction until I was certain that I was going the wrong way and then following my markers back and turning 90 degrees and heading in that direction.--The riverbed idea seemed like the best idea because it was downhill walking and that's the one I chose.

Creativity doesn't come out of thin air. To create, you have to have materials and tools to create with. When you create sentences while speaking, the better understanding that you have of the meanings of the words you are using, the more possible sentences you can create. In 3D art, you can create a lot of interesting things out of wet clay, but you can make even more unique things if you use gold leaf or bronze in conjunction with that clay, or you apply glaze to the clay. When you throw in an array of clay working tools you open up even more possibilities for the things you can create. Think of this process as fleshing out your creativity. If you have a need and it's urgent, your next task is to take stock of what materials you can use, and maybe even experiment with those materials so that you know just how useful they are. The better understanding you have of the tools and materials that you can use, the more creative you will be. If that means buying a battery and a bunch of wire, resistors, capacitors, and the like just to dabble in electronics, don't think about it, just do it. At the same time as you are being creative, you will also gain experience.

Somewhere in the process of thinking about your need and stressing to yourself how urgent that need is--and even putting yourself into more and more anxious situations that reinforce the urgency of that need--Yes, after you have taken inventory of what possible materials and tools you have access to and maybe even experimented with combining those materials together, then you will reach a moment of sudden clarity. This is what is called a Eureka moment.

Suddenly, as if from out of nowhere, your mind will create the start of an idea. From there, you can flesh it out further using the materials that you have with you to make it better and refine the idea. Sometimes we come up with good ideas but the creation of those ideas in the real world doesn't work because they defy current universal laws, much like M. C. Escher's "Waterfall," or this optical illusion:

The creativity is there, but in order to use these ideas in the real world we have to turn back to our original understanding of the individual building materials and the tools that we have on hand. If that's the case with any of your ideas, simply continue to flesh them out until you reach the Eureka moment and you really have something creative.

3. **Be Active**

Until you have reached the safety and security that is out there in the future-world, don't stop moving forward. Imagine, in a world full of robots and automation to take care of all of your needs there is a high level of safety. Anything that you don't possess now, you can easily obtain it in that world. If any problems arise, all you have to do is exercise your creative mind, come up with a solution, and have your robots manufacture the solution.

If you're reading this book, I'm assuming that you aren't in that safe place yet. You have bills to pay, you're hungry, you're tired, your frustrated by things that other people have control over. You probably aren't aware of many of the tools available to you. You probably are still like an infant, scrambling to understand how you got into the position you are in in the future-world that you were thrust into.

Rather than becoming more and more anxious about your present situation, start moving forward.

To be active is to always be working towards your future. As I said in the beginning of this book, the world is in a changing state. It hasn't settled on its final resting place after these massive quakes altered its world. Practically everyone around you is in the same situation as you are, drowning in the flood that we call now. If you stop swimming for just a moment, there is a chance that you will sink, there is a chance that you won't evolve, adapt, or live to see what the future has in store for you. Your goal, right now, is to reach safety. Safety is the future, it is that vision of stability, of a utopia where robots do all the hard work and leave you to do the fun.

Where you are now is a place of anxiety. Anxiety is good, it amplifies the urgency of your situation. Don't wait around for things to work themselves out, because they won't. Don't hold out for good fortune, because the odds are not in your favor. Don't wait around for someone else to come up with a plan for you, because you have to pay for fortune and favor and for someone to tell you what to do. It is a very costly expense to put your human evolution off; instead, start now.

Where do we go from here?

As I said, don't wait for someone to tell you what to
do, just start doing it--start being creative and solve
your own problem. Let me restate this: the problem
before you is that if you keep going in the direction
you are going, you will be forced to take jobs that
you cannot support yourself on--whether because
you physically aren't able, mentally you can't
manage it, or emotionally it's too stressful. There is
a very real danger that you might not be able to
support yourself and your family in the next 10 to
20 years. --Solve that problem.

I have given you 1 tool: how you can force
creativity and solve your own problems. Now, I'm
going to give you another tool that I think is one of
the motivating factors in your purchasing this book.
I'm going to give you step by step instructions on
how you can stop living the outdated, under-
evolved life that you have been living, and--over a
very short period of time--adapt to start living in the
new world. I'm going to give you a little bit of
intelligence and teach you how to survive and be
one of the fittest, so here goes:

This is a step by step guide to starting your own
business, being your own boss, and ultimately doing
<u>exactly</u> what you are passionate about in life. Again,
remember that ultimately no matter what you do,

you will fall into one of the 7 professions that I outlined earlier in this book.

Step 1: Flesh out your idea.

Exercise your creativity and come up with one of the following: a product, a service, or a tool that solves someone else's problem.

A **product** is a "tangible" object that can be traded on the market. I put the word "tangible" in quotes because digital objects can be products as well. For example, a 4 minute recording of a song is a product regardless of its format (CD, Digital download, live stream only, etc).

A **service** is a set of actions that you perform to create a result. For example, using your tools on hand to record a song that a musician has commissioned you to record is a service. Services tend to assist in the creation of products.

A **tool** is something that other people will use to perform services or create products. For example, software that allows you to manipulate music is a tool. Tools can be general, such as a hammer which can be used in many situations for many purposes, or highly specific, such as a robotic exoskeleton to help people maneuver who have limited mobility.

This sounds easier than it really is. Creating products, services, or tools can be exhausting, and putting your mind and body into a creative state for a prolonged period of time can take a toll on you in many ways.

If you don't already have something in mind by the time you have read this sentence, let me give you a little bit of orientation:

A. Start with something you are passionate about. What is the first thing that comes to mind when I ask you, **"What do you value most in life?"** For many people, the answer is simple: money, family, relationships, their life, music, art, so on and so forth. Now answer this, **"What is the biggest possible threat for the thing you value most?"**

If you said money, the biggest threat might be having to declare bankruptcy, or your bank shutting down and taking all of your money with it. From there, you can find a problem that affects others: being forced to declare bankruptcy is a problem for not only you, but millions of people. Think of ways that you can make "bankruptcy" easier for them that fall into either products, services, or tools, whether that's avoiding bankruptcy, going through the process of bankruptcy, or living life after bankruptcy. For this hypothetical situation, a product could be refinancing their home--essentially you buy the loan out from under them, lower the monthly payments on the balance by either giving them a lower interest rate or extending the loan, and instead of the bank taking their money, you get to collect interest on the money you lend them. A service could be assisting them in selling their car and transitioning into riding public transit and your reward for helping them could be taking a service fee off the top of each car or each asset of theirs that you sell. A tool could be better budgeting software that holds them accountable for where their money goes and automates things that they struggle with.

If your response to the first question was "family," do some research into protective services and foster care in your area. Many governments offer incentives for taking on foster children or will outright pay you. Or, perhaps you like to design weddings, or do photography at weddings. Maybe you like babies and are willing to offer a service to parents with newborns in which you stay in their home with the baby while both parents work. Or perhaps you could invent a tool that helps parents keep track of their children in case of emergencies.

The possibilities are endless, and best of all, you will be doing what you are passionate about.

B. If you aren't passionate about any one thing, then try asking other people what they are most concerned about. The idea for this book came largely from me asking friends on social media about things that bother them--lack of good jobs--and it prompted me to do some research; I asked questions about what was at the root of their problem and came to conclusions. Ultimately, I realized that there is nothing stopping anyone from having their dream job-- others have already paved the way in providing products, services, and tools; and because of the competitive global market, the price of those tools and services have dropped substantially and are available to virtually everyone.

Step 2: Hire a designer

For the rest of this chapter, I'm going to run through a hypothetical scenario as though you have an idea for a miniature pump--useful in water fountains and other applications. Obviously not all products will apply to some of the specifics that I'm going to touch on in this chapter, but I'm going to use this example because I think it highlights the specifics of how you can turn your idea into a reality.

I hinted at this a few times throughout this book that in the future, even though there are 7 job types out there, you'll probably have to be a little bit of all of them to some extent. No, you don't need to be an expert at them, but you do need to understand the basis of each job and focus on making one of them your strength.

First, you need to build a blueprint of the object.-- Use your creative abilities to make some sketches of the specific parts so that you can show it to someone else. Use your accounting and inventorying skills to write up a list of resources you'll need to create a prototype--things like a plastic shell, copper wire, etc. and show how each part of the object functions in the whole.

Next, you need to hire a designer who can turn your sketches into a 3D CAD model--for those of you who don't know what that is, CAD stands for Computer Aided Design. Think of it as a form of 3D digital art. CAD models are similar to the blueprints you would see for a house, but they are stored digitally on the computer which means they can be incredibly accurate and they can be used by other programs on the computer.

The reason we want a CAD model of your pump at this point, is for the next step; where we'll have someone else make it for us, and they might live thousands of miles away from us but we won't lose any time or money in sharing the blueprints because we can just email them a CAD file instead of several pages of blueprints. Not to mention that having it in a standardized format such as CAD helps us visualize what we imagined in the beginning. It will also prevent us from having merely a good idea that isn't practical in the real world.

How do we find a CAD designer? --Online of course! I've included a chapter in this book called, "Resources," with the specifics of websites you can use to find people willing to do this kind of work, as well as terms useful when looking for those people. We have a term for these class of people, they are called, "Freelancers," and freelancers are found everywhere in the world. They are essentially people just like you who don't want to, or can't find work within a company. Of course, there are also professional companies out there that are in the business of this very thing if you feel that you need the collective support of multiple people to accomplish this task.

**Note: Not all of your ideas are going to need a CAD design, but the point of this step is to get you to realize that you can *outsource* design work and technical work for your product, service, or tool.

You might be wondering at this point how you can pay for all of this, and if so, I have provided information and resources in the next chapter, "How do I pay for all of this?", on how you can come up with the money to pay for what you are about to do.

Step 3: Pay Someone to Build your Prototype

The same way that you found someone to design your product is the same way that you can find someone to build your prototype of that product. At this point, you just need one. You need to make sure it works the way it was designed and the get an idea for how much it is going to cost you to produce more copies of the product when you go to sell it, as well as the turnaround time for how quickly they can be made.

There are a few options for having someone build a prototype. With your CAD design, you can find someone who owns a 3D printer and can "print" all of the plastic or metal parts for you, or you can find another artist who specializes in a particular medium such as metal molds or screen printing or welding, to build it for you. Again, the internet is your friend. There are people all around the world who know the many intricacies of working with a particular resource and by having those people build your prototype for you, you not only get the finished prototype, but you also get their knowledge about the process--you can ask them questions before and after that will be useful for when you are ready to sell the product to other people.

If your idea is complex, you may want to consider hiring several people to build each part separately and when they mail the smaller parts back to you, you can assemble them yourself and inspect the quality of their work.

This has three immediate benefits:
First, because they are all working simultaneously, you will get your prototype done more quickly. Most people (robots too!) can only work on one task at a time, so by having several people work on several tasks and completing them at about the same time means you don't waste any time. Regardless, you'll still shell out roughly the same amount of money, except you'll provide jobs for multiple people instead of one person.
Second, by hiring multiple people, you get to test the individual out on a trial basis. If one person doesn't provide the level of quality you were expecting or you have a hard time working with their personality, then you know not to work with them again, and instead of your whole product being ruined, only a small portion of the product will need to be done again. This saves you money.
Third, you can keep your idea secret. When not everyone sees the big picture and is only assigned to create one small part of it, it is more difficult for them to put two-and-two together and realize the full potential of what they are doing. You essentially keep them in the dark until you are ready to reveal your product and then by that point it is

too late for them to steal your idea because you will already have sold the product.

Typically, stealing ideas isn't as much of an issue in the world of business as people think it is. You've probably heard outlandish stories about how someone had a brilliant idea and another person came in and stole the idea and pushed it to market and made all of the money off of it. That rarely happens, if ever, and usually it only happens between two well-established big businesses. Right now, you're a virtual nobody on the playing field. No one suspects anything out of you and even if they thought you had a good idea, there is a principle in the business world that the first person to market isn't the one who makes the most profit. Usually, the company that comes second or third or fourth makes a better product and captures more of a market share. They do this by looking at what works and what doesn't work from the original product and improving on it in some crucial way. They want you to push your product to the market, prove that it is useful and that people will buy it, and then they'll invest in the product. Actually, because most respectable businesses realize that you put hard work into a product, they also know that you are the most experienced person regarding the product. Businesses are more likely to buy out your business than they are to steal your ideas, and that's an even better outcome for you, isn't it?

[[As a side note, you can use this principle to your advantage while trying to come up with ideas: look for products, tools, or services that only do half of the job or that don't quite meet their customer's expectations, then improve on those products and you'll win their customers over. This lowers your risks because you already know that people are willing to pay for the product and at what relative price. You make some improvements and you already know at what price they are willing to pay for it or can justify why your product costs slightly more than the original creator's.]]

Again, when you have someone, probably clear across the world in Ukraine or Siberia or a small town in Missouri, USA make parts for your prototype, the only costs to you are the materials they use, plus what they tack on for what they think their time, energy, and experience is worth (and depending on where they live, many people will charge less because their cost of living is less) and then you'll also pay a small fee to have it shipped to you when they are done. --Take those things into consideration along with how experienced the individual is when you make a decision about who to award the building contract to.

Step 4: Record a video of your product in action

This is really just for marketing purposes. Buy whatever supplies you need and then use your cellphone to make a video of your product in action. With your assembled water pump, show people what the pump looks like, how to install it, and then turn it on and show them what it does; specifically show what is unique about it as compared to other pumps out there.

You can (and should) exercise your creativity here. If your pump is unique because it uses very little energy, attach a wattminder to it, if it is extra powerful, show in your video just what it is capable of; and if you can make it humorous, that's even better!--set it up on a switch so that is sprays unsuspecting passer bys from a long distance away.

Step 5: Hire a video editor

Most people don't have the tools (video editing software and a powerful enough computer), or don't have the time, or more importantly don't have the skills to edit videos. Again, resort to hiring freelancers. Yes, it costs money, but think of this: every time you hire someone, you create a job for another human being. Alternatively, you could buy a robot to do all of this work for you, and by robot, I mean a simple machine such as a 3D printer to manufacture your parts. Your end goal is to get a product, service, or tool that you can sell, and anything along the way that takes up your time, or that you don't like doing, you are outsourcing to someone else to do. Everyone is different and some people love doing the things that you don't know how or don't want to do--those people will do a better job at it than you will, trust me.

Furthermore, your video is going to be the first thing that your potential customers see. If it looks shotty and poorly pieced together, they'll wonder if your product is also shotty and poorly pieced together. If, however, you have a well made video and everything about your presentation looks nice, they'll treat you as though you are like any other company out there--even though you're a one person show (plus maybe a few robots).

Step 6: Share your video online

Oh how I wish I knew this the first few business ventures I started! Sharing your video online isn't as simple as having an awesome video and putting it online and having your friends share it. --I wish it were that simple!

No, sharing your video is only about 1% of where you'll get your customers. Plan now to advertise, and it's going to cost you some money. You may even decide to hire someone to set up a marketing plan for you. This can be a very tricky, confusing, and even cutthroat activity, so depending on your competition and what your product is, seriously consider hiring a consultant to set up a marketing plan for you. If you do hire someone, pay them an upfront amount and then tell them you'll give them a % share of the first X amount of units that you sell--that will give them an incentive to do a good job, but always check their credentials before hiring them. Marketers and salespeople are very slick, so be careful! Regardless of who you hire, you still have a lot of legwork that only you can do in answering a few questions about your product, so keep reading.

To help you get started, I'm going to give you a few of the basics that I know, and maybe this will be enough for you to manage on your own.

1. First and foremost, you have to define your Target Market. Answer the question, "Who will buy my product?" [or service or tool]. Be as specific as possible about what you know. And you may have multiple targets--in the case of a water pump, "who will use it and what is it for?" People use water pumps to run outdoor fountains that circulate water because stagnant water can cultivate bad bacteria. They use small pumps in aquariums and even hydroponic gardens, what groups of people have aquariums or hydroponic gardens?

"How easy is it to use your product?" In the case of a pump, you have to consider not only flipping the switch and turning the pump on, but also installing the pump--which also falls under the broad category of "using the pump." If it is difficult to use the product, then maybe only professionals will use it, or maybe you will need to include the parts and instructions to make it easier for them to install. The simpler it is to use, the more people who you will be able to target.

Consider this, professional installers only make up a small percentage of the people who use a product. In marketing we differentiate these people as Consumers, who use the product, and Customers, who purchase the product. Sometimes the professional installer is the customer and the consumer is their customer and you may have to please both of these people in order to get your product sold, so take into consideration everything you know about who will use the product, why they are using it, and be as specific as you possibly can because that will help you later down the road.

2. Once you know who you want to target, you have to set up what is called a Marketing Campaign. Basically, you need to create a plan for "how you are going to reach those people and make them aware of your new product." If your target customer's don't typically use the internet, then internet marketing is a waste of

your time and money, but there are many other avenues for where you can advertise. In the example of our mini pump, the internet is an okay location for marketing, but so might be the back of popular gardening and aquarium magazines.

Creating a marketing plan requires a lot of research. If you've never heard of or seen a gardening magazine, you would be ahead to buy one at your local grocery store, but even that isn't extensive! From my own experience having a love of gardening, seed companies mail out extensive magazines once or twice a year (before spring planting time and fall harvest time) with a list of all of the potential seeds you can purchase. Mailing these magazines costs them money and they aren't opposed to splitting the costs of printing those magazines with other advertisers. Basically, you can call or email them and ask if they want to partner with you by allowing you to put a coupon in the back of their magazine advertising your product and that you will pay them to do so. Since you aren't a direct competitor to them and they are getting reimbursed to do so, they will be more likely to agree to partnering with you. Other avenues are amongst popular bloggers and websites that your potential customers might visit (such as blogs about maintaining your aquarium). It's also important to note that you don't always have to pay people to get them to advertise your product, many bloggers will review your product and promote your product on their site if you simply give them your product for free and they like it.

When you make your marketing campaign, you want to keep account of how much money you are spending and how many potential customers you are reaching. If you use one of the many large internet marketing firms they will provide you with data that spells all of this out for you, and many will tell you exactly how many of those people respond to your ad by clicking on it. If you set up a campaign with them based on what is called Cost Per Click you are essentially only paying them when someone clicks on your ad. Check out the Resources chapter for more information on this.

While you are marketing, it's not a bad idea to split your budget in two and create two similar, but different, ads and market them the same way. This is called A+B Testing--essentially the point of this kind of testing is to help you polish your Marketing Copy, or the words and/or images you use in your ad. You are essentially running a mini science experiment to determine which is better and using the lesser one as your control. After it becomes apparent that one is less effective than the other, you can get rid of that ad and pour the rest of its budget into the ad that is most effective.

The two most important tasks you need to accomplish with your marketing campaigns are: First, to get your product and company out in front of people, this is called Branding, or making people aware of your brand, what you stand for, and what benefit your product is to them. Second, you need to determine how much it will cost you to get just 1 customer. If it costs you $5 to get 500 clicks on your ad and only 1 of them is interested enough to purchase from you, then you need to add roughly $5 to the purchase price of your product to make up for what it costs you to market it.

3. While you are marketing your product, you need to bear in mind a simple procedure called the Customer Requisition Chain (or I've heard it called by several other names), basically, there are steps to getting your product sold. The first step is to make the individual aware of your product, because without awareness they won't know that your product is out there for them to purchase. Next, you need to get them to realize how it can help them or why they need it. Third, you need to give them all of the information they need to know in order to purchase it, such as where to buy it, how much it will cost them, whether they have financing options, and basically all the rules regarding purchasing it. Fourth, (or sometimes third, second or even

first, depending on your product) they need to be given you sales pitch--which is just a call to action that incites them to buy the product.-- Again, if you're struggling with all of this you can hire a salesperson or artist/writer to write the pitch for you and even present the pitch for you if necessary. Finally, you need to get the customer to sign on the dotted line or hand over their money. At that point, you have secured 1 customer.

This is an important procedure because you can track where your customers are in the chain. If a person becomes aware of your product, then realizes that it really will help them, but they still don't have the motivation to purchase (because your pitch isn't strong enough), or they don't understand how to purchase (Because your e-commerce system is confusing or because your financing plan doesn't work for them, or because something is broken somewhere), then you know what needs your attention. You essentially have to hold each and every customer's hand along the way until they give you their money, and this is especially important in the beginning stages that we're still in. In the best requisition systems, the customer spends less than 5 minutes going from start (becoming aware) to finish (giving you their money). If you can present your product in such a good light that they fully understand how it can benefit them and they can imagine the urgent need to get it right now, you can even get people to impulse buy your product in 30 seconds--which is what infomercials do.

4. It seems like I'm getting ahead of myself here, but I'm really not. You need to take into consideration this whole process even before you post your video online, because it may change some things for you and require you to add certain bits of information in your video, such as your sales pitch or how they can purchase your product, or what applications it can be used for.

5. Finally, and this so far has all been a very basic overview of marketing, you have to post your video, create your advertisements, and link everything together to your video or your e-commerce website, or your store page. --Again, this will make more sense when we get to the Resources chapter, but basically you need to funnel every customer (in as few steps as possible) to where they will make the purchase and give you their money. That may mean they click on an ad that takes them to > your video, which they watch and then click a link that takes them to > your online store, where they add the product to their cart, check out, and then > enter their credit card information and then your order is submitted. If you can shorten that to something like, click ad > go to store and watch

video and add product to cart > enter credit card information--then that is even better!

Step 7: Create Packaging and Distribution

Now that you're all set to find customers and get their money, you have to consider how you're going to deliver (called Distribution) your product. Sure, you'll probably just stick it in the mail and they'll get it when they get it, but don't underestimate the power of distribution or the power of packaging.

Packaging sets an expectation to your customers of the quality of the product and even sometimes how they can best use the product. Furthermore, packaging can be subtle marketing--someone can stumble upon an empty box with your product's name and picture on it and decide that they too want to buy it. Packaging also protects the product in transit from damage. You can go with the most basic route and put it in a USPS flat rate box with bubble wrap, but it can still get damaged because it's not tight, and you're missing out on the subtle marketing that I mentioned earlier.

How do we create packaging? --Easy! Hire someone to do it for you or have robots build it. --In fact, probably robots will build the cardboard box and a human will design the front for you.

Step 8: Sell a few, then scale

Scaling means growing bigger. When you first start out, you only have a prototype, and hopefully it's a working prototype. After you've fixed any problems with it and you need to start producing it, but producing these products costs money and if you don't sell them then you are out whatever it costs to produce them--something that you probably can't afford starting out.

Instead, hire the same people (or different ones if you prefer) to remake all of the parts they did for the prototype. Tell them, when you hire them (again) that you would like to continue working with them and will probably have them make more of these in the future. You can possibly negotiate with them to do the work for a cheaper price because A) they know exactly what they are doing this time around, and B) there is potential for them to make more money off of you.

When you sell your first few products, make sure that your customers know that it will take you some time to manufacture and test the product. You should have a general idea of how long it took to make the first one and you can tell your customer a rough estimate of the time it takes. Also, let them know that you're still a new company and be upfront about that you want to make sure everything is done right. Most people will understand and will appreciate the time and care that you put into them and their product. What this does for you is gives you time to hire (or re-hire) people to make your product, for you to assemble and test it, and then to ship it to your customer. It's not a bad idea to periodically give your customers updates on your progress. You can tell them when you got all the parts in, once it's assembled and tested, and when you stick it in the mail to be sent to them.

After you have sold several of your products you can consider streamlining the process and growing your company. Depending on what you are selling and the tools you need, this is going to be different, but if you need a 3D printer to print plastic parts, consider purchasing one if, in the long run, it will be cheaper than paying someone else to print the parts. If you need to hire someone to do a specific function in the company (like accounting, or quality control, or assembly) then do so if it's going to save you money or time in the long run. Don't be afraid to hire other people to do the work for you or to purchase robots to do it for you. You could even pay your 13 year old neighbor to assemble the products after school for an hour each day and only have to pay him or her in cash under the table (until you get really really big).

Just remember that the price you charge your customers is going to be whatever it costs you to make and sell the product (including your average marketing costs, equipment costs, fees you pay to people that helped make it and equipment costs averaged out to the lifetime of the equipment) plus an amount that you want to keep for your hard work in inventing and managing the product.

Lastly, although I wrote this out in the example of creating products, the same rules apply for tools, which are essentially products that professionals and non-professionals use to perform tasks, or perform them better. Tools can be some of the better products to sell because when other people are making money using the tools they have greater incentive to buy better tools, and with some tools (such as software), you can "lease" the tool to them on a monthly basis either through a monthly subscription or access fee. What that means is that you can create the product once and yet continue to make money off of the product until it ceases to be useful or wears out.

With services, you'll use a lot of the same principles as you do with products, but services tend to be one-time and are largely dependent on your abilities. If you're not very good, or you have a lot of competition, it can be harder to sell your services. Not to mention that you can only sell one service at a time because there is only so much time in a day. Even still, to market your services you probably need to hire artists to make logos and advertisements for you and even to deliver those advertisements to potential customers.

The whole point of this chapter is really to get you thinking about how easy it is to be doing entirely what you love to do with your life. You can make a career out of only doing the things you enjoy doing and paying someone else, or having a robot, do the hard parts.

How do I pay for all of this?

The question that this chapter is really asking is: How do I finance this venture. Because, after all, this is a business venture. I explained early on how robots are going to do all of our work, and yes, that's true now and will be more and more true in the future, and who knows but maybe at some point robots will be doing so much that it will make our concept of money useless. For now though, you need to find a way to pay for the start-up costs of this business.

If you do all of this in the way I suggested, step by step, I'm guessing that you will need anywhere from $500 to $2,000 to get started for most basic products or tools. To some people that sounds like a lot, to others that seems like pocket change. I came at that number by estimating that each step of the process is going to cost from $50 to $250 [Go heavy on your advertising budget originally]. When you get to the Resources chapter of this book, you'll realize that I'm not exaggerating by much, you can easily make products or tools for that price, and you can cut down the costs associated with buying tools and creating services to less than $2,000. And, since you will be initially running off of a build-it-as-you-sell-it model, you don't need to lock up any money in inventory that isn't already sold.

That said, here is a list of ways you can get $2,000 in America. I'm sure if you live outside of the US the rules are similar, but I'm not familiar with how they work abroad and what will be different. Use whichever you are most comfortable or any combination of all of them and that you can mentally justify using.

1. Save the money. $2,000 spread out over 12 months is $167 per month. Make some sacrifices like canceling your gym membership and media streaming services and instead jog to the library to check out books, DVDs, and music. Walk where you can instead of using gas, and quit going out to eat in favor of buying and making food from the grocery store. The easiest way to save more money is to cut out your wants and stick to just your needs. Of course, if you have extra time, you could get a part-time job, but I'm assuming that you don't want to do that or can't do that because some robot, somewhere, has taken your part time job.
2. Beg for money. Ask your friends and family for money. You may or may not need to explain to them what you intend to do with it, but sometimes it works to just say that you neeeeed it.
3. Borrow money from friends or family. If begging doesn't work, try borrowing the money from friends or family. You don't need to borrow all of it from the same person, you can

borrow $100 from 20 people and you'll have $2000. To sweeten the deal for them, you can offer to give them interest or do them favors for lending the money now. People are usually pretty reasonable if you make it worth their while, telling someone that you'll give them $120 later in the year if they give you $100 now carries more weight than asking if you can borrow $100 and not knowing when or how you'll pay them back.

4. Sell some of your valuables. That diamond ring, gold necklace, your old guitar, cameras, old cell phones, stereo systems, unused appliances, your spare mattress--they are all worth something. You can go to the local pawn shop and pawn them, or you can sell them on classifieds websites.

5. Crowdfund. It's the 21st century, there are two ways to crowdfund: the traditional way, or the new way online. Traditionally, people crowdfunded by holding a party or get together and asking the attendees to donate to the cause. A business could hold a dinner, then during the dinner they pitch the business idea and why they need money, and at the end they ask attendees to donate. Of course they also charge money for the dinner, which usually has a significant markup to also garner in some additional money. Imagine spending $500 on a catered meal for 20, charging everyone $50 a plate, and then also bringing in another $1000 in

donations.

The modern way of crowdfunding happens online. You create a short video describing what you're doing, how much money you need, and what you'll do with the money. You offer donors an incentive (much like they would get a plate of food if they attended a traditional event) and then you release it out into the world and share it with your friends. If you choose to crowdfund online, you may need to pay for advertising just to generate buzz and build up awareness of your crowdfunding event, but the good news is that online crowdfunding sites tend to have snowball effects--after so many people donate, more people are likely to donate simply because the first person did.

6. Apply for (or use) a credit card. Credit cards are easy to get, but the interest rates on them are usually pretty high, so make sure that whatever you use your credit card for that you pay it off as quickly as possible to avoid any extra interest. Do some research because some cards come with postponed interest plans, like 6 months no interest if paid in full. If your product is simple enough, you can gamble on being able to sell your first few units before you have to pay interest on your card. If you do use this method, I recommend that you save an additional $500 in cash, just in case you need more months to pay the bill in full. The interest

on $2,000 can add up quickly and they'll expect you to pay it off with your cash on hand.

7. Borrow against your assets. If you own a car, RV, or other vehicles, you can get a title loan-- basically you can borrow up to a % of the value of that car. If you don't pay it back in the time limit they keep the title to your car and therefore own your car. They'll probably sell it at that point and you'll be without a car. Again, you'll need to pay them interest to do this.

8. Cash out your investment/retirement plan. Some investment plans allow you to cash out early, or borrow against the funds that are in them, such as a 401k. The same principles apply here as they do when you are borrowing against your assets.

9. Payday loans. Payday loans are unsecured but they sometimes have huge interest rates and lots of fees. In total, if you go this route, expect to pay $200 for every $100 you borrow.

10. Home Equity Line of Credit (HELOC). If you own a home and are paying on the mortgage, you can borrow against the equity you have already gained in the home. The interest rates are usually lower than your first mortgage, but the interest rates are variable and can go up or down depending on the market (usually up). HELOCs are a good option if you're not borrowing much or you are able to pay it back in a short amount of time. HELOCs work very

similarly to how credit cards work in that you can borrow money at any time up to the limit.

11. Home equity loan. Again, if you own a home you can borrow against the equity, but this kind of loan gives you the total amount up front (let's say $2000) and makes you pay interest plus a principal payment each month.

12. Business Microloans. Some government agencies as well as private companies specialize in offering what are called "microloans" or loans that are specifically for business startups that usually cost less than $5,000. Just like any other time you borrow money from someone, you have to pay it back, and if you go through a government organization there may be a lot of red tape involved, but the interest rates can be reasonable and if you can't get money some other way this can be a good option.

13. Look for investors. Legally in the US you can't publicly ask everyone to invest in your startup. You can privately ask people to invest, but not to strangers. There are ways that you can turn strangers into acquaintances though very quickly provided that you have an "in." Usually, your "in" is that you know one of their friends or family members. Let me share with you who you should be looking for:
Right now (2016) there are a lots of people of retirement age that have accumulated a lot of money over the years through the stock market, pension plans, insurance, and they probably

have a lot of assets as well. If you don't have good credit, money, or means but you have a good idea, you can approach these people and ask for a personal loan from them. Yet again, you'll have to present to them why you need the money, how much money, how soon you can get it back to them, what they will gain from investing, and probably they'll want to know about who you are and if you're reliable and good on your word. Sometimes these people want a share in the business--i.e., they'll want a cut of your profits for the lifetime of the business (or at least until they sell their share of it to you or to a 3rd party). Best of all, if you get investors this way, they will be more likely to help you if you struggle with your business because they own a share of the potential profits. Other times you can convince them to issue a personal loan that works just like a bank loan. --You can cut any kind of deal with investors that you feel is reasonable, just remember to put it down on paper and have the both of you sign it before exchanging the money.

If your situation is bad enough, or the risk is incredibly high, you may need to offer up to 60 or 70% of the business to them just to get your idea off the ground. So how do you find these investors? It's easy, first, look around your neighborhood. Is anyone retired or of that age that they may retire soon? Second, do you have any friends that are about to retire, or are any of their parents close to retirement? Third, after speaking with your friends' parents and your neighbors, always ask them if they know anyone who, like them, is close to retirement and may be looking for investment opportunities. They can refer you to their friends and family who in turn could invest. --This applies to both those people who choose to invest, and those people who choose not to invest. This is called networking, and each referral you get gives you permission to legally approach them and ask them if they will help you get your business off the ground.

14. Opt into medical experiments. You can resort to donating plasma (provided you are healthy) and you can also be part of clinical drug trials. Donating plasma takes about 1-2 hours and can be usually be done twice a week. You basically sit in a chair while it pumps out your blood plasma and then pumps the blood back into your body. There are also medical research places willing to shell out $2,000 plus room and board to keep you in a hospital for a month and have you taking pills while they track your vitals and make you take surveys. It's not always exciting, but it's worth a shot if you have no other options.

All told, you'll probably have to do a combination of all of the above. It's not a bad idea to have 30%

in cash if you intend to use some form of credit or loan system. There are also little tricks you can do that seem completely irrelevant but land you at your ultimate goal of possessing $2,000 for your idea. For instance, at some banks, if you just maintain a certain amount of money in the bank for the period of 1 to 3 months, they will lending up to that amount in a personal, unsecured loan. You can get your first $500 by borrowing from close family at 0% interest, leave it in there for a few months and then get a personal loan for $500 from the bank (viola, you're at $1,000). Then you can approach investors and show them that you have $1,000 in your bank account and need another $1,000 investment capital. Since they can see that you already have half of what it takes, they recognize that the risk is substantially less and so they will be more willing to invest their $1,000, instead of having to invest $2,000. Meanwhile, you can be saving up $200 money of your own during the first 3 months and use that money, since it is in the form of cash, to pay the interest on the $500 personal loan you took out at the bank, which gives you more time to look for investors to get the rest of the money.

After the first 3 months, during the time that you are looking for investors, you don't actually need to keep the money in your bank account; you can start paying freelancers to begin the work for you and during the rest of your time you can be meeting with, and looking for, investors.

Start looking for financing right now, even if you don't have an idea yet. Building up a sizeable credit limit can take some time, and it's better to have a higher credit limit than you actually intend to use because: A) it looks better to creditors that you aren't pushing the limits of your credit; and B) if you ever do have an emergency, you still have wiggle room to get out of it.

Resources

Below is a list of resources you will need to familiarize yourself with. I have organized them by what they are useful for:

Hiring Freelancers and Robots
Upwork.com (formerly Odesk and Elance)
This is a useful site for hiring freelancers all across the world. Their quality, and pricing varies drastically--you can pay a very small amount of money to someone and get outstanding work, or you can pay a lot and get outstanding work. The reverse, unfortunately, is also true: you can pay a lot and get very little for your money, or you can pay a little and still not get anything.
If you can figure out how to use the system, in what places to hire cheaply and what places to really spend your money, you'll do really well with Upwork.

Fiverr.com
The beauty of this site is that most freelancers have a basic service that they offer for just $5 USD. Usually, they try to upsell you by adding add-ons for more money such as expediting your project, or making it just a little bit better (though "better" is relative). Personally, I use Fiverr for graphic design work, such as logos. The people on there tend to specialize in a certain style or type of logo, such as Vintage or 3D Text, and if you use a little bit of

your own creativity beforehand and get an idea of what you want out of a logo, then you can hire someone who has done similar work to make it for you.

3dhubs.com
Need your little invention 3d Printed? --Locally even? This is the site for you. Local printers will print your object and mail it to you--Some will even let you pick them up in person.

Useful Parts and Products
etsy.com
Maybe you don't need to hire someone, maybe all you need are materials. I put this one at the top of the list because some people on etsy will also do custom work. Some artists on etsy specialize in selling materials to make things; such as specialty ropes, leather, wood, and metal goods. It doesn't hurt to look on etsy first to see if they have some of the materials you need to make your product.

Amazon.com
Ya, ya, you've heard of the place...Amazon has basically anything you can imagine and often at a cheaper price than anywhere else. Sometimes you don't need to pay someone to make a part when you can buy the part from a distributor like Amazon. I've found that Amazon has an excellent stock of electronic parts, particularly testing equipment,

switches, and fuses from which I can build my inventions.

Ebay.com
Ebay isn't dead, though it's heyday years are long past. Ebay is still an online marketplace, and you can still buy just about anything on the site. I like ebay because sometimes people put their used items online for cheap. Used items can be repurposed or even incorporated into whatever it is I'm making. I've also found some very useful tools on there that are hard to come by elsewhere.

For Research and Learning
Google.com (and its sister sites like Youtube and GoogleMaps)
Yes, Google. Google knows everything. If you have a question, ask it on google and you'll probably find several sites that talk about it. I used google all of the time, even for simple things like how many grams are in a pound or square feet in an acre. Google tends to be one of the best starting places if you ever have a question, but to fully utilize it as a learning tool you have to keep asking questions and read through a lot of information and possibly watch a video.

Wikipedia.org
Wikipedia is another great starting place for learning. Wikipedia is considered "the people's encyclopedia." All content on wikipedia was

created by and edited by it's users rather than the site's owners, which means the information can be inaccurate at times, but the community does a good job of keeping inaccuracies to a minimum.

Your Local Library
You would be surprised at the things you can get, for free, from your local library (at least in the US). There's books, sure, but they also keep legal records, maps, and usually have a subscription to national statistics databases. Really, if you aren't using your local library you're wasting your time in so many ways. Some Libraries even have 3D printers that you can use to print prototype parts for free! Not to mention that they usually have places you can rent out to hold meetings, Audio/Video equipment, free internet, video conference capabilities, accounting software--I could create a really long list of things the library has. The good news is, if you have to make a few sacrifices so you can save up enough money over the next few months, you can always utilize those same resources at the library. I've even heard rumors of some libraries having Netflix subscriptions.

Marketing
Google Adwords Adwords is one of the big boys in the online advertising industry. Because people use google all of the time, it stands to reason that somewhere out there one of your potential customers is using google right now. Adwords uses

keywords to isolate individuals who are more likely to check out your ad. If you use Adwords, just remember, they are getting paid to get people to click on your ad--you still have to convince those ad-clickers to buy your product on your own; Adwords can only get them to your site or to view your video, it's up to you to get them the rest of the way through your requisition chain.

Facebook Ads
Facebook ads are similar to Google Adwords, but facebook targets people in a different way. They base who they show ads to around certain characteristics of that individual's account. Sometimes this is really accurate and sometimes it is limited by what information the individual provides on their facebook account. In any case, use the best advertising method that's going to more accurately reach your target market.

LinkedIn Ads
Linkedin does offer advertising--a lot of people don't realize that--but bear in mind who uses linkedin and what is on their mind when they use it: professional business. If you're targeting business professionals, Linkedin can be great and can be very specific about who it shows your ads to. Whenever you advertise, bear in mind what things your potential customers will be thinking about when they stumbled on your ad--if they are in the mindset already for what you are selling, they will

be much more likely to click on your ad and take an interest in your product, otherwise they'll just ignore your ad or if they click on it and find out that it isn't something they are interested in, then you waste your money from having them click on it. This advice goes towards Linkedin, Facebook, and Google.

Twitter Ads Twitter also offers ads, though their ads are more like amplified tweets. There is a specific time and place for these kinds of ads, again, if you know for certain that your potential customers will be on twitter thinking about things related to your product, service, or tool, then go ahead and used Twitter's ads.

There are a lot of possibilities for how you can reach your target market, you just have to be creative. Try to put yourself in the shoes of someone who would benefit from your product and think of ways that you can insert yourself into their daily routine at the exact moment that they are wondering about topics related to your product.

Financing
Paypal
Paypal is basically an online bank. They offer tools for accepting payments, as well as sending payments. Additionally, you can use paypal's credit system, bill me later, which allows you to purchase products at 0% interest for the first 6 months if you

pay it off in 6 months. To use paypal, you have to have an account and to purchase things on credit, the company/person you purchase from has to as well. Your customers don't have to have an account, they can check out using a guest paypal account.

Paypal charges you a fee for accepting credit cards or ACH payments (direct from the bank), but not your customers. You can pad your price by a rough equivalent of paypal's fee. Certain services are free, such as transferring from paypal to paypal (useful for paying freelancers), so look into their terms for any ways you can save money.

Dwolla
Dwolla is another form of internet banking, much like paypal. Dwolla specializes in ACH transactions, or bank to dwolla and dwolla to bank transactions. They charge a very low fee (even lower than paypal) for each transaction across customers/accounts, so if you want to pay a freelancer, dwolla can be an excellent option.

Amazon Payments
Not only can you list your products on amazon, you can also utilize the ease of checkout that is found at Amazon on your own website. Amazon Payments allows people to purchase your products using their Amazon account, and these days so many online shoppers have Amazon accounts that it seems like a no-brainer to include it on your site.

Kickstarter

Kickstarter is a crowdfunding website. They take a % cut for using their website to crowdfund, and they have specific rules regarding what you can or can't do with the money, but if you follow their rules and are fine with giving them a cut, Kickstarter is a great source of funds. Kickstarter adds a degree of credibility to your crowdfunding-- the rules in place and the approval process vouch for your organization's credibility. Also, the closer that you get to your goal, Kickstarter will start to recommend your campaign to complete strangers and your donations can snowball.

Indiegogo

Similar to Kickstarter but with different rules, Indiegogo is a crowdfunding site. Indiegogo tends to tap into a more global market than Kickstarter, which focuses on the American scene.

With any crowdfunding online, bear in mind that you may need to not only pay for the crowdfunding site's fees, but also external advertising to make people aware that you are seeking donations and where they go (the web address) to place those donations. Another tip I can offer you is that you secure guaranteed donors to start your campaign off with a bang even before you launch the crowdfunding campaign. Approach friends and family and get them to agree to donate on the site (not to you in person) because it aids with the snowballing effect that these sites have--yes, you will have to pay a fee to do it that way rather than accept cash up front, but it's usually worth it.

Alternatively, you can use Paypal, Amazon, and/or Dwolla on your own personal website to collect donations in a similar fashion.

Other Tools
Google Tools
I wrote the first few drafts of this book on google docs. Google has online cloud tools such as spreadsheets, presentations, gmail, and a cloud drive to store your documents, files and pictures. Best of all, the first few gigs are free! If you run out of room and love the service you can always purchase more on a monthly payment plan.

Amazon Cloud
Another cloud service that people often overlook. Amazon gives away free storage in conjunction with their memberships or purchasing a kindle from them.

Godaddy, BlueHost, HostGator
A few of the top web hosting sites. There are a lot of options, some complex, and some very simple (like wordpress-only hosting). If you know a little bit about web technology, you can probably get set up with the bare essentials that you need to host

your own site, or you can work with one of their representatives to pick the best services.

Lynda.com
Lynda.com is an online learning site. Let's say you want to learn how to program HTML, CSS, PHP, and Javascript, but don't want to get a degree in computer science. You can learn on Lynda.com and for a very low monthly subscription. Furthermore, you have access to basically every topic imaginable. --One day you might even find me on there!

Kajabi
Similar to Lynda, but user driven. You can use this site to host your own courses, or you can pay to take other people's courses. If you want to sell the service of teaching someone how to do something, or how to be better, but you know that you won't be available all of the time to hold class, you can design courses for them to complete on their own time online.

The Library
I'm not joking here, I repeated it on purpose. If you aren't utilizing at least a couple of tools or services that the library provides you're wasting your money somehow. Libraries have free internet, free access to information such as books, maps and otherwise. Many are starting to offer checkout of e-books anywhere in the world through internet download. Some are implementing 3D printers. They even

have meeting rooms for free or for low cost rental in case you need to hold a meeting.

There are so many tools out there, some of which I am aware of but didn't include in this book, and others that I'm not even aware of! Do some poking around on the internet and you'll probably stumble into free tools to accomplish whatever you need to accomplish on your shoestring budget.

Conclusion

There are big changes on the horizon, and I hope by reading this book you are suddenly aware of some ways that you can survive those changes--maybe you're even a little bit excited! These changes are not a matter of "IF," they are a matter of "WHEN" they will affect you. The events leading up to them have already happened and it's only a matter of time before you feel the impact. As you can see by the guide I have provided for you, it is easily possible for you to start your own business, change your life, and start letting others do all of the hard work for you.

Yes, there will probably always be a few jobs out there with a clear defined employer, but over the next decade you will see a sharp decline in the number of available jobs of that kind. Working for someone else offers very few benefits, in fact, I can only see one: you don't assume as many risks. But consider this: if your employer, one day, decides to cut jobs and replace you with a machine, or outsource your work to a contract in Yugoslavia, is that not a risk you are taking? Even still, working for someone else has very clearly defined drawbacks:

- You have to come into work, even when you don't want to. If you work for yourself, you have freedom to do whatever you want, whenever you want--just don't take on more contracts than you can handle and give yourself ample time to get your orders shipped or your services performed. Usually, when you work for yourself, you can shift your schedule around and work in the evening if you want to take the day off to go fishing.

- If someone else--such as your boss or a salesperson--makes a mistake, you suffer the consequences, whether that's less work to do or more work to do. You aren't the only person to blame, but you're definitely the person who suffers because of it. When you work for yourself you know that only your mistakes are counted against you.
- If they tell you to do something, you have to do it, even if you don't want to. You can't outsource your work, only your boss can outsource your job, and he or she wants you to do the hard stuff, not someone else.

As I've stated throughout this book, our entire civilization is in a transition state right now. There are still social concepts out there that in the near future will be obsolete. You might not be able to transition right away to working for yourself, and that's okay, because lucky for you, for the time being you can still do both! You can work for someone else while you are working part time at your business idea, or while you save up money to start your business. Maybe you even need some time to come up with an idea; in which case you should practice creativity every day. Try writing down 5 ideas (even if they are bad) each day, then review the previous day's five ideas and try to flesh them out further. If you find yourself thinking about one idea day after day after day, that's the one-- work on that idea until it's good, and in the meantime be saving up money every where you can.

It bothers me that so many people will complain about not having money to do what they want with their life. I've heard plenty of people tell me that they need money to travel the world and I have always laughed at that idea. You can travel the world for free, and probably make a lot of money doing it. The problem is that people don't want to do it the free way--they don't even want to prepare and plan for the free way!--they want a free pass to luxury instead. Life doesn't work that way--especially not in the 21st century. If you want something, you should change your lifestyle to accommodate it. Sell all your possessions, buy a backpack, some basic essentials, and start walking. That's the best way to travel the world. If you get hungry, invest in a book on wild plants you can eat, or find things you can sell along the way. Maybe even write a book or take photos along the way in the process. Beg for money in every city you come to. Eat leftover food that people throw out in the trash. Hitch a ride if you get tired. Use that creative mind of yours and do something about it. Panhandlers in U.S. metro areas easily earn $100/day just by being artists on the street corner--they stimulate other humans into feeling a certain emotion and then accept payment for that stimulation. Even if you only did it one 8 hour period for every city you come to, you could easily afford to go to a grocery store and get cheap supplies, a national gym membership can provide you with a shower and locker, and the library grants you access to email, the internet, and a whole slew of tools.

Don't waste any more time than you have to. If you aren't at least planning for this drastic change, and working towards your plans, then you'll probably always have something to complain about because there will always be things that come up that prevent you from doing what you want to do with your life--that's what happens when you don't leap quick enough towards those things you want in life; other things come in and fill their place. Yes, you have time before this massive social transition takes place, but to be honest, you're already far behind.

Be prepared for the future. In the future, robots and computers will do just about everything for us--as they should. One day, money will become irrelevant, because there will be no need to buy anything when our personal robots can build it for us and accumulate the resources we need. If you want fresh orange juice, a machine will squeeze you orange juice produced from fruit that your robotic garden grew and harvested for you. If you need to go somewhere, your single-seater helicopter--piloted by computers and powered by renewable energy--will take you there.

Our current concept of money is that it is used to exchange goods or services, but the amount of money exchanged is relative. For someone who has the tools lined up in an automated system, the costs are very little, they could flip a switch and in a short amount of time they would have a finished product. If they power their machines with renewable energy, the costs are practically $0.

To further complicate matters, many of the world's currency is based on supply and demand--when someone wants something, it gives meaning and value to the currency needed to exchange for that thing. The less copies of that thing that there are, and the more people who want it, the higher that price gets inflated.

In the future, when everyone can have anything at zero cost, very few things will require money. The things of value that people will be willing to pay money for will be ideas. It's not that they can't come up with the idea themselves, it's that they don't want to or don't spend their time thinking about those creative ideas. Oddly, ideas are free and cost next to nothing and haven't costed anything for ages. People will be willing to pay exorbitant amounts of money for your ideas which cost you next to nothing to come up with simply because they don't want to think of those things themselves. In fact, you don't even have to wait for that future, because they'll pay you oodles of money if you can solve their problems for them even before they are problems right now.

Sadly, in the future, your multi-billion dollar ideas--that cost you next to nothing to come up with--won't be paid to you in the form of cash. Cash will be useless in the future because you won't need it--very few things will require money so why would you accumulate it? Instead of cash, you might exchange your ideas for other ideas or even favors; but even that will get old. You see, if you have good ideas that will help your friends, you'll help your friends for free because they are your friends. That's how it should be.

The reason that we rely so much on money right now is because our whole mindset is off. I know, I know, I told you to come up with products, services, and tools that you can sell to other people, but that model is only going to work for a finite amount of time. Eventually, there won't be products to sell because everyone will already have them. This has happened many times in the past: whole industries have collapsed because no one wanted to buy the products because they already had one or they no longer needed one. Think about how big the horse breeding industry was until cars started being mass produced--Everyone needed a good horse until they could afford a car.

There are little tricks here and there that people use when inventing products that limit the usefulness of the product or the longevity, but it seems like such a waste of human innovation. If you have the chance to make a useful product that will last a very long time, do it, even if you lose out on money because of it. Ideas are free, and once you know how to be creative you can get ideas very easily. Ideas are the new currency and if you have them then you are already very wealthy, you just need to know how to tap into that wealth.

Final Notes

Thanks for reading my book. I hope you're as excited about the future as I am. I'm full of ideas and I, like so many other people, get frustrated that ideas never seem to be enough in this world. I wrote this book thinking that it would help people who have good ideas get the motivation to implement their ideas.

In case you're wondering, yes, I did follow all of my own advice when creating this book. It cost me nothing to write it--I even used Google Docs to write it initially because I couldn't afford to spend money on a word processing program, then I formatted it into digital format using basic web programming--I self taught myself how to program, and you can too just by reading a book at the library or browsing around online w3schools.com is an excellent starting point!--I self-published this book and followed a CPC advertising model to spread the word about it. I'm only selling it on online retailers that will print it on-demand or sell the digital copy, so any costs involved are paid for out of each and every individual unit that I sell.

When the time comes, I will offer this book for free--either at the time of my death, or when I no longer see it as necessary. You can look at your purchase as more of a donation than an actual purchase because I've committed to a new lifestyle devoted to the advancement of humankind.

Lately, I have taken a strong interest in developing renewable, 100% sustainable food and living systems. I love gardening and raising animals and am looking for ways to make a 100% sustainable farm. I enjoy writing and inventing and if you catch me working for someone else it's either because I'm saving up for my next big venture or because I am good friends with that person. If I come up with some good ideas on how to be 100% sustainable, I'll share them with the world as well--I hope you will too!

Feel free to email me if you have questions or comments regarding the book: webmaster@embracehumanity.org

--K. Oakes, a pseudonym for Kyle Oakeson

Other books I've published:

Relationship Confidence: What it takes to have a great relationship
A basic (but in depth!) book about having confidence. Confidence is the foundation for just about anything you want to do in life. If you lack confidence your whole life can feel out of whack. This book takes an analytical approach to what confidence is and how you can improve your confidence.

Opportunities and Threats: Dealing with Relationship Risks
Risk management is the principle of weighing the chances of both good and bad outcomes and then making decisions that boost the chances of a good outcome but diminish the possibility of a bad outcome. I outline ways you can improve your relationships with other people in this book just by doing things that take advantage of good opportunities and limit your stakes on threats to your relationship.